LET THIS DASH DIET COOKBOOK HELP YOU

LOSE WEIGHT NATURALLY USING 50 SIMPLE BUT HEALTHY RECIPES

Table of Contents

Introduction

DASH diet or Dietary Approaches to Stop Hypertension is a lifetime method to healthy eating. This diet program is intended to prevent hypertension whilst encourage one to take on the low sodium diet.

What to eat?

Here's a rundown of the suggested serving sizes for a 2,000 calorie DASH diet.

Grains – this includes bread, pasta, and rice. Whole grains are recommended because they contain more nutrients and fiber weigh against the refined version. For instance, eat brown rice, whole-wheat pasta, and whole-grain bread instead of white rice, regular pasta, and white bread. When shopping for food, always look for 100% whole wheat and whole grain.

In a day, you're allowed to eat grains of at least one serving, ½ cup cereal (cooked), one slice of whole wheat bread, ½ cup pasta, or ½ cup rice.

Fruits – you are allowed to consume at least 4 servings in a day. You may portion your fruit consumption by snacking ½ cup of fresh fruits in the morning, a serving of 1 medium-sized fruit in the afternoon, and 4 ounces any fruit juice of choice as an afternoon snack, and another ½ cup of canned or frozen fruit in the evening. For fruit juices, make sure that you go for freshly squeezed ones. If you're buying canned fruits, ensure that there is no sugar added.

Vegetables – 4 servings are allowed in the Dash diet. Example servings include 1 cup of cooked or raw vegetables. Both frozen and fresh vegetables are excellent vegetable sources. However, when you buy canned or frozen veggies, make sure that they are low in sodium. In order to increase the number of servings of vegetables in a day, you have to be creative in your cooking. In the morning, you may have stir-fried mixed vegetables, during lunch time, you can have steamed vegetables, fresh carrots and celery sticks during snack time, and vegetables with a slice of chicken breast for dinner. Just remember to double up the amount of veggies instead of meat.

Protein – you can go for poultry, lean meat, and fish. It is advised that you consume at least 4-6 servings of any of these. Opt for the leaner versions and servings should be no more than 6 oz in a day. For cooking, grilling, baking, and broiling instead of frying are suggested.

Dairy – you can have at least 2 servings of this in a day. If you're going to have milk, cheese, or yogurt, ensure that they are fat free or low in fat. Example serving is 1 cup skim milk, 1 1/2 oz cheese (part-skim) or 1 cup yogurt (low fat).

Whether you're already doing the DASH diet or you're still planning to do it, here are some tips on how to get started and stay on track:

1. List everything before you head to the supermarket

If you want to be consistent in your diet, everything should begin with your food. So before you go to the grocery, it is important that you:

- Create a checklist - this includes all the meals and ingredients that you're going to make for the coming days or for a whole week. It would also be easier to indicate if the meal is for breakfast, lunch, dinner, or snacks. With all these listed, it's less likely that you'll grab unhealthy food.

- Make sure your stomach is full before heading to the grocery – this is because when you go there hungry, all food that you see will look appealing to you especially those high in sodium and fat.

2. Always keep the DASH diet in mind

When going grocery shopping, it is but normal to be tempted to go to bargain sales, but just as you would want to get a discount on these, most food on this rack are prohibited in the Dash diet as they are mostly sugary and have too much salt.

3. Always go for the fresh ones

Most food that are high in sodium are the processed ones. Fresh food are definitely healthier options because only a little sugar, fat, and sodium are added. Fresh food also contain natural vitamins and minerals weigh against the frozen, canned, and processed ones.

4. Make it a habit to read the labels all the time

The Nutrition facts at the back of each food item is there for good reason. When reading labels, look for reduced fat and sodium products. Choose the ones lower in fat and sodium, and those with fewer calories.

5. Shop the sides

Fresh produce, lean meats, and low-fat products are always found at the sides. Those at the center aisles are mostly prohibited in the dash diet.

Recipes

Breakfast

1 Easy Quinoa Pancakes

Preparation time: 10 minutes

Cooking time: 6 minutes

Servings: 8

Ingredients:

½ cup unsweetened applesauce

2 tablespoons coconut sugar

½ cup nonfat milk

1 tablespoon lemon juice

1 teaspoon baking soda

1 and ½ cups quinoa flour

Directions:

In your food processor, combine the applesauce with the sugar, milk, lemon juice, baking soda and quinoa and pulse well.

Heat up a pan over medium heat, spoon some of the pancake batter, spread into the pan, cook for 3 minutes on each side and transfer to a plate.

Repeat with the rest of the pancake batter, divide the pancakes between plates and serve for breakfast.

Enjoy!

Nutrition: calories 188, fat 3, fiber 6, carbs 13, protein 6

2 Quinoa And Egg Muffins

Preparation time: 10 minutes

Cooking time: 30 minutes

Servings: 3

Ingredients:

1/3 cup quinoa, cooked

1 zucchini, chopped

2 eggs

4 egg whites

½ cup low-fat feta cheese, shredded

A pinch of black pepper

A splash of hot sauce

Cooking spray

Directions:

In a bowl, combine the quinoa with the zucchini, eggs, egg whites, cheese, black pepper and hot sauce, whisk well and divide into 6 muffin cups greased with the cooking spray. Bake the muffins in the oven at 350 degrees F for 30 minutes. Divide the muffins between plates and serve for breakfast.

Enjoy!

Nutrition: calories 221, fat 7, fiber 2, carbs 13, protein 14

3 Apple And Quinoa Breakfast Bake

Preparation time: 10 minutes

Cooking time: 10 minutes

Servings: 6

Ingredients:

1 cup quinoa, cooked

¼ teaspoon olive oil

2 teaspoons coconut sugar

2 apples, cored, peeled and chopped

1 teaspoon cinnamon powder

½ cup almond milk

Directions:

Grease a ramekin with the oil, add quinoa, apples, sugar, cinnamon and almond milk, stir, introduce in the oven, bake at 350 degrees F for 10 minutes, divide into bowls and serve. Enjoy!

Nutrition: calories 199, fat 2, fiber 7, carbs 14, protein 8

4 Quinoa Patties

Preparation time: 10 minutes

Cooking time: 20 minutes

Servings: 6

Ingredients:

2 and ½ cups quinoa, cooked

A pinch of black pepper

4 eggs, whisked

1 yellow onion, chopped

¼ cup chives, chopped

1/3 cup low-fat parmesan, grated

3 garlic cloves, minced

1 cup whole wheat bread crumbs

1 tablespoon olive oil

Directions:

In a large bowl, combine the quinoa with black pepper, eggs, onion, chives, parmesan, garlic and bread crumbs, stir well and shape medium patties out of this mix.

Add quinoa patties, cook them for 10 minutes on each side on a heated pan with the oil over medium-high heat, divide them between plates and serve for breakfast. Enjoy!

Nutrition: calories 201, fat 3, fiber 4, carbs 14, protein 8

5 Peanut Butter Smoothie

Preparation time: 10 minutes

Cooking time: 0 minutes

Servings: 2

Ingredients:

2 tablespoons peanut butter

2 cups non-fat milk

2 bananas, peeled and chopped

Directions:

In your blender, combine the peanut butter with the milk and bananas, pulse well, divide into 2 glasses and serve.

Enjoy!

Nutrition: calories176, fat 4, fiber 6, carbs 14, protein 7

6 Yogurt Peanut Butter Mix

Preparation time: 10 minutes

Cooking time: 0 minutes

Servings: 3

Ingredients:

6 ounces nonfat yogurt

2 tablespoons red grapes, halved

4 teaspoons grape jelly

1 tablespoon fat-free peanut butter

1 teaspoons peanuts, chopped

Directions:

In a bowl, combine the yogurt with the grapes, grape jelly, peanut butter and peanuts, toss well, divide into small cups and serve for breakfast. Enjoy!

Nutrition: calories 187, fat 2, fiber 3, carbs 6, protein 8

7 Slow Cooked Oatmeal

Preparation time: 10 minutes

Cooking time: 8 hours

Servings: 3

Ingredients:

4 cups nonfat milk

2 cups steel cut pats

4 cups water

1/3 cup raisins

1/3 cup cherries, dried

1/3 cup apricots, dried and chopped

1 teaspoon cinnamon powder

Directions:

In your slow cooker, combine the milk with the oats, water, raisins, cherries, apricots and cinnamon, stir, cover, cook on Low for 8 hours, divide into bowls and serve for breakfast. Enjoy!

Nutrition: calories 171, fat 3, fiber 6, carbs 15, protein 7

Soup

8 Potato and Asparagus Bisque

Preparation time: 5 minutes

Cooking Time: 6 minutes

Serving: 4

Ingredients:

1 ½ pound asparagus

2 pounds sweet potatoes

6 cups vegetable broth

1 large sized onion

8 cloves garlic

2 tablespoons dried dill

2 tablespoons flavored vinegar

3-4 cups almond milk

4 tablespoons Dijon mustard

4 tablespoons yeast

Directions:

Add the listed ingredients (except milk, mustard and yeast) to your pot.

Lock the lid and cook on HIGH pressure for 6 minutes.

Release the pressure naturally.

Open the lid and add almond milk, yeast and mustard.

Puree using immersion blender.

Serve over rice.

Enjoy!

Nutrition:

Calories: 430

Fat: 12g

Carbohydrates: 77g

Protein: 6g

9 Cabbage and Leek Soup

Preparation time: 10 minutes

Cooking Time: 25 minutes

Serving: 4

Ingredients:

2 tablespoons coconut oil

½ head chopped up cabbage

3-4 diced ribs celery

2-3 carefully cleaned and chopped leeks

1 diced bell pepper

2-3 diced carrots

2/3 cloves minced garlic

4 cups chicken broth

1 teaspoon Italian seasoning

1 teaspoon Creole seasoning

Black pepper as needed

2-3 cups mixed salad greens

Directions:

Set your pot to Sauté mode and add coconut oil.

Allow the oil to heat up.

Add the veggies (except salad greens) starting from the carrot, making sure to stir well after each vegetable addition.

Make sure to add the garlic last.

Season with Italian seasoning, black pepper and Creole seasoning.

Add broth and lock the lid.

Cook on SOUP mode for 20 minutes.

Release the pressure naturally and add salad greens, stir well and allow to sit for a while.

Allow for a few minutes to wilt the veggies.

Season with a bit of flavored vinegar and pepper and enjoy!

Nutrition:

Calories: 32

Fat: 0g

Carbohydrates: 4g

Protein: 2g

10   Onion Soup

Preparation time: 10 minutes

Cooking Time: 3 hours

Serving: 4

Ingredients:

2 tablespoons avocado oil

5 yellow onions, cut into halved and sliced

Black pepper to taste

5 cups beef stock

3 thyme sprigs

1 tablespoon tomato paste

Directions:

Take a pot and place it over medium high heat.

Add onion and thyme and stir.

Reduce heat to low and cook for 30 minutes.

Uncover pot and cook onions for 1 hour and 30 minutes more, stirring often.

Add tomato paste, stock and stir.

Simmer for 1 hour more.

Ladle soup into bowls and enjoy!

Nutrition:

Calories: 200

Fat: 4g

Carbohydrates: 6g

Protein: 8g

11   Carrot, Ginger and Turmeric Soup

Preparation time: 15 minutes

Cooking Time: 40 minutes

Serving: 4

Ingredients:

6 cups chicken broth

¼ cup full fat coconut milk, unsweetened

¾ pound carrots, peeled and chopped

1 teaspoon turmeric, ground

2 teaspoons ginger, grated

1 yellow onion, chopped

2 garlic cloves, peeled

Pinch of pepper

Directions:

Take a stockpot and add all the ingredients except coconut milk into it.

Place stockpot over medium heat.

Bring to a boil.

Reduce heat to simmer for 40 minutes.

Remove the bay leaf.

Blend the soup until smooth by using an immersion blender.

Add the coconut milk and stir.

Serve immediately and enjoy!

Nutrition:

Calories: 79

Fat: 4g

Carbohydrates: 7g

Protein: 4g

12   Split Pea cream Soup

Preparation time: 10 minutes

Cooking Time: 15 minutes

Servings: 6

Ingredients:

2 tablespoons olive oil

1 chopped yellow onion

½ cup chopped celery

18 oz, low-salt chicken stock

2 cups water

½ cup coconut cream

1 pound chicken sausage, ground

½ cup chopped carrots

2 minced garlic cloves

black pepper for taste

16 oz, split peas, rinsed

¼ teaspoon dried pepper flakes

Directions:

Press sauté mode and add sausage, browning for 2-3 minutes then transferring to plate.

Add oil to IP, then add celery, onions, carrots, water, garlic, stock, pepper flakes, and peas, stirring, and cooking on manual for 10 minutes.

Blend with an immersion blender and then sauté once more, and add the pepper, sausage, and corn, simmering and mix it all together.

Nutrition: Calories: 281, Fat: 7g, Carbs: 19g, Net Carbs: 7g, Protein: 16g, Fiber: 12g.

Poultry

13   Teriyaki Chicken Wings

Preparation time: 15 minutes

Cooking time: 30 minutes

Servings: 6

Ingredients:

3 pounds of chicken wings (15 – 20)

1/3 cup lemon juice

¼ cup of soy sauce

¼ cup of vegetable oil

3 tablespoons chili sauce

1 garlic clove, finely chopped

¼ teaspoon fresh ground pepper

¼ teaspoon celery seed

Dash liquid mustard

Directions:

Prepare the marinade. Combine lemon juice, soy sauce, chili sauce, oil, celery seed, garlic, pepper, and mustard. Stir well, set aside. Rinse and dry the chicken wings.

Pour marinade over the chicken wings. Coat thoroughly. Refrigerate for 2 hours. After 2 hours. Preheat the broiler in the oven. Drain off the excess sauce.

Place the wings on a cookie sheet with parchment paper. Broil on each side for 10 minutes. Serve immediately.

Nutrition: Calories - 96 Protein - 15g Carbohydrates - 63g Fat - 15g Sodium-145mg

14   Hot Chicken Wings

Preparation time: 15 minutes

Cooking time: 25 minutes

Servings: 4

Ingredients:

10 - 20 chicken wings

½ stick margarine

1 bottle Durkee hot sauce

2 Tablespoons honey

10 shakes Tabasco sauce

2 Tablespoons cayenne pepper

Directions:

Warm canola oil in a deep pot. Deep-fry the wings until cooked, approximately 20 minutes. Mix the hot sauce, honey, Tabasco, and cayenne pepper in a medium bowl. Mix well. Place the cooked wings on paper towels. Drain the excess oil. Mix the chicken wings in the sauce until coated evenly.

Nutrition: Calories - 102 Protein - 23g Carbohydrates - 55g Sugars - 0.1g Fat - 14g Sodium-140mg

15   Crispy Cashew Chicken

Preparation time: 15 minutes

Cooking time: 30 minutes

Servings: 5

Ingredients:

2 chicken breasts, skinless, boneless

2 egg whites

1 cup cashew nuts

¼ cup bread crumbs

2 cups of peanut oil or vegetable oil

¼ cup of corn starch

1 teaspoon brown sugar

2 teaspoons salt

1 teaspoon dry sherry

Directions:

Warm oven to 400 F. Put the cashews in a blender. Pulse until they are finely chopped. Place in a shallow bowl and stir in the bread crumbs.

Wash the chicken breasts. Pat them dry. Cut into small cubes. In a separate shallow bowl, mix the salt, corn starch, brown sugar, and sherry. In a separate bowl, beat the egg white.

Put the oil into a large, deep pot. Heat to high temp. Place the chicken pieces on a plate. Arrange the bowls in a row; flour, eggs, cashews & bread crumbs. Prepare a baking tray with parchment paper.

Dunk the chicken pieces in the flour, then the egg, and then the cashew mixture. Shake off the excess mixture. Gently place the chicken in the oil. Fry on each side for 2 minutes. Place on the baking tray.

Once done, slide the baking tray into the oven. Cook for an additional 4 minutes, flip, cook for an additional 4 minutes, until golden brown. Serve immediately, or cold, with your favorite low-fat dip.

Nutrition: Calories - 86 Protein - 21g Carbohydrates - 50g Sugars - 0.1g Fat - 16g Sodium-139mg

16   Chicken Tortellini Soup

Preparation time: 15 minutes

Cooking time: 30 minutes

Servings: 5

Ingredients:

2 chicken breasts, boneless, skinless; diced into cubes

1 Tablespoon flavorless oil (olive oil, canola, sunflower)

1 teaspoon butter

2 cups cheese tortellini

2 cups frozen broccoli

2 cans cream of chicken soup

4 cups of water

1 large onion, diced

2 garlic cloves, minced

2 large carrots, sliced

1 celery stick, sliced

1 teaspoon Oregano

½ teaspoon Basil

Directions:

Pull the broccoli out of the freezer. Set in a bowl. Rinse and pat dry the chicken breasts. Dice into cubes. In a large pot, heat the oil. Fry the cubes of chicken breast. Pull from the pot, place on paper to drain off the oil.

Add the teaspoon of butter to the hot pot. Sauté the onion, garlic, carrots, and celery, broccoli. Once the vegetable el dente, add the chicken soup and water. Stir the ingredients until they are combined. Bring it to a simmer.

Add the chicken and tortellini back to the pot. Cook on low within 10 minutes, or until the tortellini is cooked. Serve immediately.

Nutrition: Calories - 79 Protein - 15g Carbohydrates - 55g Sugars - 0g Fat - 13g Sodium-179mg

17   Chicken Divan

Preparation time: 15 minutes

Cooking time: 30 minutes

Servings: 4

Ingredients:

1/2-pound cooked chicken, boneless, skinless, diced in bite-size pieces

1 cup broccoli, cooked, diced into bite-size pieces

1 cup extra sharp cheddar cheese, grated

1 can mushroom soup

½ cup of water

1 cup croutons

Directions:

Warm oven to 350 F. In a large pot, heat the soup and water. Add the chicken, broccoli, and cheese. Combine thoroughly. Pour into a greased baking dish. Place the croutons over the mixture. Bake within 30 minutes or until the casserole is bubbling, and the croutons are golden brown.

Nutrition: Calories - 380 Protein - 25g Carbohydrates - 10g Sugars - 1g Fat - 22g Sodium-397mg

Seafood

18   Lemony Mussels

Preparation time: 5 minutes

Cooking time: 5 minutes

Servings: 4

Ingredients:

2 pound mussels, scrubbed

2 garlic cloves, minced

1 tablespoon olive oil

Juice of 1 lemon

Directions:

Put some water in a pot, add mussels, bring to a boil over medium heat, cook for 5 minutes, discard unopened mussels and transfer them to a bowl.

In another bowl, mix the oil with garlic and lemon juice, whisk well, add over the mussels, toss and serve.

Enjoy!

Nutrition: calories 140, fat 4, fiber 4, carbs 8, protein 8

19   Greek Salmon with Yogurt

Preparation time: 10 minutes

Cooking time: 15 minutes

Servings: 4

Ingredients:

4 medium salmon fillets, skinless and boneless

1 fennel bulb, chopped

Black pepper to the taste

¼ cup low-sodium veggie stock

1 cup non-fat yogurt

¼ cup green olives pitted and chopped

¼ cup chives, chopped

1 tablespoon olive oil

1 tablespoon lemon juice

Directions:

Arrange the fennel in a baking dish, add salmon fillets, season with black pepper, add stock, bake in the oven at 390 degrees F for 10 minutes and divide everything between plates.

In a bowl, mix yogurt with chives, olives, lemon juice, olive oil and black pepper and whisk well.

Top the salmon with this mix and serve.

Enjoy!

Nutrition: calories 252, fat 2, fiber 4, carbs 12, protein 9

20   Salmon and Potatoes Mix

Preparation time: 10 minutes

Cooking time: 10 minutes

Servings: 4

Ingredients:

1 and ½ pounds potatoes, chopped

1 tablespoon olive oil

4 ounces smoked salmon, chopped

1 tablespoon chives, chopped

2 teaspoons prepared horseradish

¼ cup coconut cream

Black pepper to the taste

Directions:

4 Heat up a pan with the oil over medium heat, add potatoes and cook for 10 minutes.

5 Add salmon, chives, horseradish, cream and black pepper, toss, cook for 1 minute more, divide between plates and serve. Enjoy!

Nutrition: calories 233, fat 6, fiber 5, carbs 9, protein 11

21 Easy Shrimp And Mango

Preparation time: 10 minutes

Cooking time: 0 minutes

Servings: 4

Ingredients:

3 tablespoons balsamic vinegar

3 tablespoons coconut sugar

6 tablespoons avocado mayonnaise

3 mangos, peeled and cubed

3 tablespoons parsley, finely chopped

1 pound shrimp, peeled, deveined and cooked

Directions:

In a bowl, mix vinegar with sugar and mayo and whisk.

In another bowl, combine the mango with the parsley and shrimp, add the mayo mix, toss and serve.

Enjoy!

Nutrition: calories 204, fat 3, fiber 2, carbs 8, protein 8

22   Especial Glazed Salmon

Preparation time: 45 minutes

Cooking Time: 10 minutes

Serving: 4

Ingredients:

4 pieces salmon fillets, 5 ounces each

4 tablespoons coconut aminos

4 teaspoon olive oil

2 teaspoons ginger, minced

4 teaspoons garlic, minced

2 tablespoons sugar-free ketchup

4 tablespoons dry white wine

2 tablespoons red boat fish sauce, low sodium

Directions:

Take a bowl and mix in coconut aminos, garlic, ginger, fish sauce and mix.

Add salmon and let it marinate for 15-20 minutes.

Take a skillet/pan and place it over medium heat.

Add oil and let it heat up.

Add salmon fillets and cook on high heat for 3-4 minutes per side.

Remove dish once crispy.

Add sauce and wine.

Simmer for 5 minutes on low heat.

Return salmon to the glaze and flip until both sides are glazed.

Serve and enjoy!

Nutrition:

Calories: 372

Fat: 24g

Carbohydrates: 3g

Protein: 35g

Vegetarian and Vegan

23   Glazed Eggplant Rings

Preparation time: 15 minutes

Cooking time: 10 minutes

Servings: 4

Ingredients:

3 eggplants, sliced

1 tablespoon liquid honey

1 teaspoon minced ginger

2 tablespoons lemon juice

3 tablespoons avocado oil

½ teaspoon ground coriander

3 tablespoons water

Directions:

1. Rub the eggplants with ground coriander. Then heat the avocado oil in the skillet for 1 minute. When the oil is hot, add the sliced eggplant and arrange it in one layer.

2. Cook the vegetables for 1 minute per side. Transfer the eggplant to the bowl. Then add minced ginger, liquid honey, lemon juice, and water in the skillet. Bring it to boil and add cooked eggplants. Coat the vegetables in the sweet liquid well and cook for 2 minutes more.

Nutrition: Calories 136 Protein 4.3g Carbohydrates 29.6g Fat 2.2g Sodium 11mg

24   Sweet Potato Balls

Preparation time: 15 minutes

Cooking time: 10 minutes

Servings: 4

Ingredients:

1 cup sweet potato, mashed, cooked

1 tablespoon fresh cilantro, chopped

1 egg, beaten

3 tablespoons ground oatmeal

1 teaspoon ground paprika

½ teaspoon ground turmeric

2 tablespoons coconut oil

Directions:

1. Mix mashed sweet potato, fresh cilantro, egg, ground oatmeal, paprika, and turmeric in a bowl. Stir the mixture until smooth and make the small balls. Heat the coconut oil in the saucepan. Put the sweet potato balls, then cook them until golden brown.

Nutrition: Calories 133 Protein 2.8g Carbohydrates 13.1g Fat 8.2g Sodium 44mg

25   Chickpea Curry

Preparation time: 15 minutes

Cooking time: 10 minutes

Servings: 4

Ingredients:

1 ½ cup chickpeas, boiled

1 teaspoon curry powder

½ teaspoon garam masala

1 cup spinach, chopped

1 teaspoon coconut oil

¼ cup of soy milk

1 tablespoon tomato paste

½ cup of water

Directions:

1. Heat coconut oil in the saucepan. Add curry powder, garam masala, tomato paste, and soy milk. Whisk the mixture until smooth and bring it to boil.

2. Add water, spinach, and chickpeas. Stir the meal and close the lid. Cook it within 5 minutes over medium heat.

Nutrition: Calories 298 Protein 15.4g Carbohydrates 47.8g Fat 6.1g Sodium 37mg

26   Pan-Fried Salmon with Salad

Preparation time: 15 minutes

Cooking time: 20 minutes

Servings: 4

Ingredients:

Pinch of salt and pepper

1 tablespoon extra-virgin olive oil

2 tablespoon unsalted butter

½ teaspoon fresh dill

1 tablespoon fresh lemon juice

100g salad leaves, or bag of mixed leaves

Salad Dressing:

3 tablespoons olive oil

2 tablespoons balsamic vinaigrette

1/2 teaspoon maple syrup (honey)

Directions:

1. Pat-dry the salmon fillets with a paper towel and season with a pinch of salt and pepper. In a skillet, warm-up oil over medium-high heat and add fillets. Cook each side within 5 to 7 minutes until golden brown.

2. Dissolve butter, dill, and lemon juice in a small saucepan. Put the butter mixture onto the cooked salmon. Lastly, combine all the salad dressing ingredients and drizzle to mixed salad leaves in a large bowl. Toss to coat. Serve with fresh salads on the side. Enjoy!

Nutrition: Calories 307 Fat 22g Protein 34.6g Sodium 80mg Carbohydrate 1.7g

27   Veggie Variety

Preparation time: 15 minutes

Cooking time: 15 minutes

Servings: 2

Ingredients:

½ onion, diced

1 teaspoon vegetable oil (corn or sunflower oil)

200 g Tofu/ bean curd

4 cherry tomatoes, halved

30ml vegetable milk (soy or oat milk)

½ tsp curry powder

0.25 tsp paprika

Pinch of Salt & Pepper

2 slices of Vegan protein bread/ Whole grain bread

Chives for garnish

Directions:

1. Dice the onion and fry in a frying pan with the oil. Break the tofu by hand into small pieces and put them in the pan. Sauté 7-8 min. Season with curry, paprika, salt, and pepper. The cherry tomatoes and milk and cook it all over roast a few minutes. Serve with bread as desired and sprinkle with chopped chives.

Nutrition: Calories 216 Fat 8.4g Protein 14.1g Sodium 140mg Carbohydrate 24.8g

---

Side Dishes, Salads & Appetizers

28　Garlic Zucchini Fries

Preparation time: 10 minutes

Cooking time: 20 minutes

Servings: 4

Ingredients:

4 zucchinis, cut into medium fries

A pinch of black pepper

½ teaspoon chili powder

1 tablespoon olive oil

¼ teaspoon garlic powder

Directions

Spread the zucchini fries on a lined baking sheet, add black pepper, chili powder, garlic powder and oil, toss, introduce in the oven, bake at 400 degrees F for 20 minutes, divide between plates and serve as a side dish.

Enjoy!

Nutrition: calories 185, fat 3, fiber 2, carbs 6, protein 8

29   Tahini Beans

Preparation time: 10 minutes

Cooking time: 10 minutes

Servings: 4

Ingredients

1 and ½ tablespoons tahini paste

Juice of 1 lemon

Zest of 1 lemon, grated

2 tablespoons olive oil

1 garlic clove, minced

1 red onion, sliced

1 yellow bell pepper, sliced

10 ounces green beans, halved

A pinch of black pepper

Directions:

In a bowl, mix lemon zest, lemon juice, tahini and black pepper and whisk well.

Heat up a pan with the oil over medium-high heat, add onion, stir and cook for 5 minutes.

Add the bell pepper, garlic and green beans, toss and cook for 10 minutes.

Add tahini dressing, toss, cook for 2 minutes more, divide between plates and serve as a side dish.

Enjoy!

Nutrition: calories 180, fat 10, fiber 6, carbs 13, protein 8

30   Mustard Tarragon Beets

Preparation time: 10 minutes

Cooking time: 0 minutes

Servings: 5

Ingredients:

1 tablespoon Dijon mustard

1 and ½ tablespoon olive oil

8 ounces beets, cooked and sliced

2 tablespoons tarragon, chopped

A pinch of black pepper

Directions:

In a bowl, mix mustard with oil and black pepper and whisk.

In a bowl, combine the beets with the tarragon and the mustard mix, toss, divide between plates and serve as a side dish.

Enjoy!

Nutrition: calories 170, fat 5, fiber 7, carbs 8, proteins 10

31   Almond Beans

Preparation time: 10 minutes

Cooking time: 20 minutes

Servings: 6

Ingredients:

5 tablespoons olive oil

3 pounds green beans, halved

8 tablespoons almonds, toasted and sliced

A pinch of black pepper

2 yellow onions, chopped

2 and ½ tablespoons parsley, chopped

Directions:

Heat up a pan over medium-high heat, add green beans, cook them for 5 minutes and transfer to a bowl.

Heat up the same pan with the olive oil over medium heat, add onions and a pinch of black pepper, stir and cook for 10 minutes.

Add beans, almonds and parsley, toss, cook for 5 minutes, divide between plates and serve as a side dish.

Enjoy!

Nutrition: calories 130, fat 1, fiber 2, carbs 7, protein 6

32   Tomatoes Side Salad

Preparation time: 10 minutes

Cooking time: 0 minutes

Servings: 4

Ingredients:

½ bunch mint, chopped

8 plum tomatoes, sliced

1 teaspoon mustard

1 tablespoon rosemary vinegar

A pinch of black pepper

Directions:

In a bowl, mix vinegar with mustard and pepper and whisk.
In another bowl, combine the tomatoes with the mint and the
vinaigrette, toss, divide between plates and serve as a side
dish.

Enjoy!

Nutrition: calories 70, fat 2, fiber 2, carbs 6, protein 4

33   Squash Salsa with Cilantro

Preparation time: 10 minutes

Cooking time: 13 minutes

Servings: 6

Ingredients

3 tablespoons olive oil

5 medium squash, peeled and sliced

1 cup pepitas, toasted

7 tomatillos

A pinch of black pepper

1 small onion, chopped

2 tablespoons fresh lime juice

2 tablespoons cilantro, chopped

Directions:

Heat up a pan over medium heat, add tomatillos, onion and black pepper, stir, cook for 3 minutes, transfer to your food processor and pulse.

Add lime juice and cilantro, pulse again and transfer to a bowl.

Heat up your kitchen grill over high heat, drizzle the oil over squash slices, grill them for 10 minutes, divide them between plates, add pepitas and tomatillos mix on top and serve as a side dish.

Enjoy!

Nutrition: calories 120, fat 2, fiber 1, carbs 7, protein 1

34   Apples And Fennel Mix

Preparation time: 10 minutes

Cooking time: 0 minutes

Servings: 3

Ingredients:

3 big apples, cored and sliced

1 and ½ cup fennel, shredded

1/3 cup coconut cream

3 tablespoons apple vinegar

½ teaspoon caraway seeds

Black pepper to the taste

Directions:

In a bowl, mix fennel with apples and toss.

In another bowl, mix coconut cream with vinegar, black pepper and caraway seeds, whisk well, add over the fennel mix, toss, divide between plates and serve as a side dish.

Enjoy!

Nutrition: calories 130, fat 3, fiber 6, carbs 10, protein 3

35   Roasted Celery

Preparation time: 10 minutes

Cooking time: 25 minutes

Servings: 3

Ingredients:

3 celery roots, cubed

2 tablespoons olive oil

A pinch of black pepper

2 cups natural and unsweetened apple juice

¼ cup parsley, chopped

¼ cup walnuts, chopped

Directions:

In a baking dish, combine the celery with the oil, pepper, parsley, walnuts and apple juice, toss to coat, introduce in the oven at 450 degrees F, bake for 25 minutes, divide between plates and serve as a side dish.

Enjoy!

Nutrition: calories 140, fat 2, fiber 2, carbs 7, protein 7

36   Thyme Spring Onions

Preparation time: 10 minutes

Cooking time: 40 minutes

Servings: 8

Ingredients:

15 spring onions

A pinch of black pepper

1 teaspoon thyme, chopped

1 tablespoon olive oil

Directions:

Put onions in a baking dish, add thyme, black pepper and oil, toss, bake in the oven at 350 degrees F for 40 minutes, divide between plates and serve as a side dish.

Enjoy!

Nutrition: calories 120, fat 2, fiber 2, carbs 7, protein 2

37   Carrot Slaw with Dijon Mustard

Preparation time: 10 minutes

Cooking time: 10 minutes

Servings: 4

Ingredients:

¼ yellow onion, chopped

5 carrots, cut into thin matchsticks

1 tablespoon olive oil

1 garlic clove, minced

1 tablespoon Dijon mustard

1 tablespoon red vinegar

A pinch of black pepper

1 tablespoon lemon juice

Directions:

In a bowl, mix vinegar with black pepper, mustard and lemon juice and whisk.

Heat up a pan with the oil over medium heat, add onion, stir and cook for 5 minutes.

Add garlic and carrots, stir, cook for 5 minutes more, transfer to a salad bowl, cool down, add the vinaigrette, toss, divide between plates and serve as a side dish.

Enjoy!

Nutrition: calories 120, fat 3, fiber 3, carbs 7, protein 5

Dessert and Snacks

38   Peach and Bacon Appetizer

Preparation time: 2 minutes

Cooking time: 0 minutes

Servings: 2

Ingredients:

1 peach, cut into 8 wedges

8 bacon slices

Directions

Roll 1 peach wedge in 1 bacon slice, wrap, and arrange on a platter.

Repeat with the rest of the ingredients and serve as an appetizer. Enjoy!

Nutrition: Calories 180, fat 2, fiber 5, carbs 11, protein 9

39   Garlic Sesame Dip

Preparation time: 2 minutes

Cooking time: 0 minutes

Servings: 6

Ingredients:

1 cup sesame seed paste

1 cup veggie stock

½ cup lemon juice

½ teaspoon cumin, ground

3 garlic cloves, chopped

Directions

In a blender, mix the sesame paste with the stock, lemon juice, cumin and garlic, pulse very well, divide into bowls and serve.

Enjoy!

Nutrition: Calories 170, fat 12, fiber 2, carbs 12, protein 6

40   White Bean Spread

Preparation time: 10 minutes

Cooking time: 7 hours

Servings: 4

Ingredients:

1 cup white beans

1 teaspoon apple cider vinegar

1 cup veggie stock

1 tablespoon water

Directions

In your slow cooker, mix beans with stock, stir, cover, cook on Low for 6 hours, drain, add vinegar and water, pulse well using an immersion blender, divide into bowls and serve as a party spread.

Enjoy!

Nutrition: Calories 196, fat 6, fiber 5, carbs 11, protein 7

41   Tropical Fruit Salad

Preparation time: 15 minutes

Cooking time: 0 minutes

Servings: 4

Ingredients:

1 cup fresh pineapple chunks

½ cup chopped orange

½ cup chopped, dried papaya

1 banana, sliced

½ cup unsweetened, flaked coconut

1 cup low-fat yogurt

1 medium piece crystallized ginger, finely chopped

1 teaspoon vanilla

Dash of nutmeg

Direction

Combine all the fruit and the coconut. Mix the yogurt, ginger and vanilla together and stir into the fruit. Top with a dash of nutmeg.

Nutrition 153 calories 5g fat 4g protein 24g carbohydrates 48mg sodium 102mg potassium

42   Vanilla Meringue Cookies

Preparation time: 5 minutes

Cooking time: 10 minutes

Servings: 6

Ingredients:

3 egg whites

½ teaspoon cream of tartar

1/3 cup sugar

1 teaspoon vanilla

1 cup unsweetened shredded coconut

1 cup sugar-free chocolate chips

½ cup chopped almonds

Direction

Preheat oven to 400°F (205°C). Beat the egg whites until frothy. Add the cream of tartar and continue beating until the meringue stands in peaks. Add the sugar gradually. Add the vanilla. With a large rubber spatula, carefully fold in the coconut, chocolate chips and almonds.

Line a cookie sheet with a silicone baking mat or parchment. Drop the mixture by spoonful onto the pan, forming cookies about the size of a large strawberry.

Put the pan in the hot oven, turn the heat off and leave the door shut. Do not remove the cookies until the oven is cold and the cookies are completely cool.

Nutrition 314 calories 20g fat 7g protein 27g carbohydrates 36mg sodium 61mg potassium

43   Brown Butter Pear Bars

Preparation time: 10 minutes

Cooking time: 40 minutes

Servings: 6

Ingredients:

2 cups crushed sugar-free cookies

½ cup unsalted butter, melted

2 eggs

½ cup brown sugar

1 teaspoon vanilla

1/3 cup flour

½ teaspoon ground ginger

¼ teaspoon baking powder

2 medium pears, cored and diced

½ cup unsweetened, flaked coconut

½ cup chopped dried apricots

Direction

Preheat oven to 350°F (180°C). In a small mixing bowl, combine crushed cookies and melted butter. Press into a lightly greased 9-inch square glass pan. Bake 20 minutes. Beat the eggs, sugar and vanilla. In a separate bowl combine flour, ginger and baking powder. Stir into egg mixture and then fold in the pears, coconut and apricots. Spread this mixture over the warm crust. Bake another 20 minutes, or until nicely browned. Cool on a rack and cut these into bars while still slightly warm.

Nutrition 295 calories 12g fat 6g protein 43g carbohydrates 149mg sodium 166mg potassium

44   Mocha Chocolate Mousse

Preparation time: 5 minutes

Cooking time: 0 minutes

Servings: 4

Ingredients:

1 (12-ounce / 340-g) package sugar-free chocolate chips

½ cup sugar

1 cup boiling black coffee

3 eggs

1 teaspoon vanilla

Direction

Combine the chocolate chips and sugar in the blender. Turn the blender on high and slowly pour in the boiling coffee. Keep the blender running and add the eggs, 1 at a time. Turn the blender to low, add the vanilla and blend another 10 seconds.

Pour the mixture into 8-ounce / 227-g glasses and set them in the freezer. You can eat this frozen, or just leave it in the freezer until it sets. Serve chilled.

Nutrition 374 calories 24.6g fat 8g protein 30g carbohydrates 202mg sodium 231mg potassium

45   Sweet Plums Mix

Preparation time: 10 minutes

Cooking time: 15 minutes

Servings: 4

Ingredients:

1-pound plums, stones removed and halved

2 tablespoons coconut sugar

½ teaspoon cinnamon powder

1 cup of water

Directions:

1. In a pan, combine the plums with the sugar and the other ingredients, bring to a simmer and cook over medium heat for 15 minutes.

2. Divide into bowls and serve cold.

Nutrition: 30calories 0.1g protein 8g carbohydrates 0.1g fat 2mg sodium 27g potassium

46   Chia Apples Mix

Preparation time: 10 minutes

Cooking time: 10 minutes

Servings: 4

Ingredients:

2 cups apples, cored and cut into wedges

2 tablespoons chia seeds

1 teaspoon vanilla extract

2 cups naturally unsweetened apple juice

Directions:

In a small pot, combine the apples with the chia seeds and the other ingredients, toss, cook over medium heat for 10 minutes, divide into bowls and serve cold.

Nutrition: 155calories 1.5g protein 33.5g carbohydrates 2.4g fat 15mg sodium 240g potassium

47   Rice Pudding

Preparation time: 10 minutes

Cooking time: 25 minutes

Servings: 4

Ingredients:

6 cups of water

1 cup of coconut sugar

2 cups black rice

2 pears, cored and cubed

2 teaspoons cinnamon powder

Directions:

Put the water in a pan, heat it over medium-high heat, add the rice, sugar and the other ingredients, stir, bring to a simmer, reduce heat to medium and cook for 25 minutes.

Divide into bowls and serve cold.

Nutrition: 340calories 2.4g protein 85.3g carbohydrates 0.8g fat 12mg sodium 191g potassium

48   Ravaging Blueberry Muffin

Preparation Time: 10 minutes

Cooking Time: 30 minutes

Servings: 4

Ingredients:

1 cup almond flour

Pinch of sunflower seeds

1/8 teaspoon baking soda

1 whole egg

2 tablespoons coconut oil, melted

½ cup coconut almond milk

¼ cup fresh blueberries

Directions:

Pre-heat your oven to 350 degrees F.

Line a muffin tin with paper muffin cups.

Add almond flour, sunflower seeds, baking soda to a bowl and mix, keep it on the side.

Take another bowl and add egg coconut oil, coconut almond milk and mix.

Add mix to flour mix and gently combine until incorporated.

Mix in blueberries and fill the cupcakes tins with batter.

Bake for 20-25 minutes.

Enjoy!

Nutrition:

Calories: 167

Fat: 15g

Carbohydrates: 2.1g

Protein: 5.2g

Sodium 13%

49   Berries Marinated in Balsamic Vinegar

Preparation Time: 10 minutes

Cooking Time: 0 minutes

Servings: 2

Ingredients:

1/4 cup balsamic vinegar

2 tablespoons brown sugar

1 teaspoon vanilla extract

1/2 cup sliced strawberries

1/2 cup blueberries

1/2 cup raspberries

2 shortbread biscuits

Directions:

Combine balsamic vinegar, vanilla, and brown sugar in a small bowl.

Toss strawberries with raspberries and blueberries in a bowl.

Pour the vinegar mixture on top and marinate them for 15 minutes.

Serve immediately.

Nutrition:

Calories 176

Total Fat 11.9 g

Saturated Fat 1.7 g

Cholesterol 78 mg

Sodium 79 mg

Total Carbs 33 g

Fiber 1.1 g

Sugar 10.3 g

Protein 13 g

50   Lemon Pudding Cakes

Preparation Time: 10 minutes

Cooking Time: 40 minutes

Servings: 4

Ingredients:

2 eggs

1/4 teaspoon salt

3/4 cup sugar

1 cup skim milk

1/3 cup freshly squeezed lemon juice

3 tablespoons all-purpose flour

1 tablespoon finely grated lemon peel

1 tablespoon melted butter

Directions:

Set the oven to heat at 350 degrees F.

Grease the custard cups with cooking oil.

Whisk egg whites with salt and ¼ cup sugar in a mixer until it forms stiff peaks.

Beat egg yolks with ½ cup sugar until mixed.

Stir in lemon juice, milk, butter, flour, and lemon peel. Mix it until smooth.

Fold in the egg white mixture.

Divide the batter into the custard cups.

Bake them for 40 minutes until golden from the top.

Serve.

Nutrition:

Calories 174

Total Fat 10.2 g

Saturated Fat 4.4 g

Cholesterol 120 mg

Sodium 176 mg

Total Carbs 19 g

Fiber 1.9 g

Sugar 11.4 g

Protein 12.8 g

Conclusion

The DASH diet also emphasizes the importance of low-fat dairy products, lean meats, beans, seeds, and nuts. Sodium (salt), saturated fats, and sweets should be eaten sparingly. When choosing whole grains make sure you purchase those that aren't processed or refined and have no added sugar, sodium or preservatives. These foods will keep you feeling full and will provide you with long-lasting energy.
When following the DASH diet, you can enjoy a variety of foods from the major food groups but in smaller portions. Eating high-fiber foods and getting adequate amounts of exercise while following the diet will help you lose weight and maintain your diet over the long term.

By following the DASH diet, you will see a significant reduction in your LDL-bad cholesterol and blood pressure levels. This may reduce your risk of developing heart disease, stroke and cancer. The DASH diet may also reduce the risk of developing kidney disease.

People can enjoy the DASH diet indefinitely or maintain a healthy weight while following the diet for about two years. When following the DASH diet sustainably, you can further reduce your risk of heart disease, high blood pressure, and obesity.

The DASH diet is designed to reduce the risk of developing chronic diseases such as heart disease, diabetes, and stroke. The diet is 55-65% carbohydrate, 30-35% fat and 10-15% protein.

The DASH Diet was really intended to help people who suffer from high blood pressure levels. Aside from reducing your sodium intake, the DASH Diet also increases your absorption of Potassium, Magnesium, and Calcium. By following this diet, you will be able to experience a drop in your blood pressure levels to a few points. And if you continually follow this diet regimen, your systolic blood pressure can go down by at the most 8 to 14 points.

The diet's aim is to consume 1,000 milligrams of sodium or less per day. About 3.8 grams per day of Fiber is consumed. A diet considered low fat contains 30-35% saturated fat, no more than 7% trans-fat, and less than 300 milligrams of cholesterol. The saturated fat portion can take the form of oils, fatty meats, full-fat dairy foods, and other animal products. Low-fat milk and low-fat cheese are good options but look for reduced-sodium versions. Salt is consumed in very small amounts.

The DASH Diet has been successful at reducing blood pressure for many, so it can be a great way to lose moderate amounts of weight, too. It has been backed by US governmental research. While it's a good diet for blood pressure, it isn't necessarily an ideal diet for weight loss. It can be great for weight loss as well, but read those studies carefully.

The DASH diet is interesting in many ways, because it is a diet that can be tailored to several lifestyles. The DASH diet, for example, suggests a healthy balance of lean meat and whole grains. However, because you will be selecting your own foods and following the weight loss plan outlined in this article, you can alter the diet to fit your own requirements. The DASH diet encourages a healthy and balanced diet for weight loss, but you only want to include foods that you are able to stick to.

Dash teaches and spurs - one of the significant reasons why individuals think that it's simple to adhere to the diet. Additionally, the eating regimen doesn't expect us to quit any pretense of anything critical in our standard diet; rather, it encourages us to make a procedure of acclimating to little changes so we can effectively support ourselves.